THE TROPHY
A WOLF STORY

KAREN WILSON

Copyright @2022 by Karen Wilson

All rights reserved. No part of this book may be reproduced in any form or by any electronic or mechanical means, including information storage and retrieval systems, without permission in writing from the publisher, except by reviewers, who may quote brief passages in a review.

This publication contains the opinions and ideas of its author. It is intended to provide helpful and informative material on the subjects addressed in the publication. The author and publisher specifically disclaim all responsibility for any liability, loss or risk, personal or otherwise, which is incurred as a consequence, directly or indirectly, of the use and application of any of the contents of this book.

WORKBOOK PRESS LLC
187 E Warm Springs Rd,
Suite B285, Las Vegas, NV 89119, USA

Website:	https://workbookpress.com/
Hotline:	1-888-818-4856
Email:	admin@workbookpress.com

Ordering Information:
Quantity sales. Special discounts are available on quantity purchases by corporations, associations, and others.
For details, contact the publisher at the address above.

Library of Congress Control Number:

ISBN-13:   978-1-952754-33-3 (Paperback Version)
           978-1-952754-35-7 (Digital Version)

REV. DATE: 25/07/2022

Introduction

Since I was a small child, you could find me outside finding something fun to do. I would sit for hours in the woods or stroll around the lake just listening to the different sounds. My father shared his love of the outdoors and my mother shared her love of life. Together they developed in me a sense of adventure to look for the truth in life's mysteries.

Telling stories about my younger years one would think I lived in a time of horse-drawn covered wagons. My stories tell of a time when I helped my father with tapping of Maple Trees to harvest syrup, my many journeys out in the woods picking wild blueberries, wintergreen, strawberries, mushrooms, and looking for that perfect agate on the shores of Lake Superior. I enjoy telling stories about a time when the air was clean, and there was no worry about the fish I caught, clean, and ate, and stories about my snowmobiling, skiing (on water or snow), and camping in all types of weather. It did not matter what nature tossed me, I would find myself outside, enjoying the seasons and having fun.

Some of the favorite stories children ask for are when I came face to face with a wild bear or a dog with rabies, or what happened when one of my Girl Scouts encountered her first skunk, but their all-time favorite story is about my first encounter with a wolf. It was this experience that gave me the idea for my story "The Trophy A Wolf Story."

At one time our fear of the wolf caused the government to place a bounty on the wolf's head. We almost brought the wolf to extinction, and if the truth be told we did wipe out the wolf in many states. Ever since there near-extinction society's thinking about the wolf has not changed much. We still tell the old stories and fables about the wolf that brings back fear into the hearts of listeners.

The wolf is important to our ecosystem and helps bring balance to this earth. Wolves are very family oriented. They show great patience in teaching their offspring survival and acceptance, no matter what skill the pup may have from the alpha to the omega. Wolves have lived among deer, elk, and moose all their lives without depleting this meat source. As a hunter, I am glad to see a wolf take down a sick or weak animal. This keeps our deer, elk, moose, and other animals strong and healthy. I love to hear howls at night when I am sitting at a campfire. This gives me the opportunity to tell stories about the wolf to our children, to celebrate them rather than teach children to fear them.

I believe people can co-exist with nature. I believe if people would take time out to experience nature, then they would not be in such a hurry to destroy it. I have a saying: "It is the fear of the unknown that leads us to do things that we would not normally do, and we are the keepers of life. We should take only what we need to live on. We should never deplete what the Lord has given us, for each living thing has a purpose. If we disrupt the balance of nature, we humans will suffer at the mercy of an unbalance world. We will no longer enjoy life as we knew it."

My experiences in nature as a child have compelled me to reach out to my readers and listeners to try to save what wildlife we have lift.

The howling of the winter wind brought with it the sounds of a lonely wolf. The Howls sent Jake and his sister Emmy closer to the warmth of the fire in their little log cabin. As the wolf continued to howl, Jake's Pa added more logs to the fire and began to tell the children stories about how the wolves robbed young children right out of their cradles; how their enormous teeth ripped right through one's flesh with ease and how their piercing yellow eyes could burn right into one's soul.

As Pa continued to speak, everyone listened. Pa always clutched the wolf's tooth necklace around his neck then took out a silver piece from his trousers pocket before telling the story of how he got his first wolf.

"It was the Devil himself. His howls kept folks up for many a night. Windows were boarded up. Doors were locked and a wave of fear ripped through our bones each time the wolf howled. The men gathered in the center of our small village. A silver piece was nailed to a wooden post by the town crier which was only to be taken down by the man who replaced it with a dead wolf.

The men's laughter and small talk kept us calm before the hunt. That wolf was clever, he was. He had the hunters running back and forth throughout those woods for days."

Pa always paused there. He never went into much detail about the actual hunt. It was as if he had more to tell. After a brief pause, Pa continued his story, but his voice became stern.

"The wolf was dead and tied to a pole. People still feared him. That didn't stop them from coming. People came from all directions just to get a glimpse of the monster who had kept them up all night with his howls. For days the wolf hung on that pole like a large trophy."

Another howl filled the room just as Pa finished his story. Ma got up from her rocker while Pa placed the silver piece back into his trouser pocket. Ma told the children that it was time for bed.

Emmy jumped into her bed and pulled the quilt over her head. Before Jake went to his bed, he started to howl.

"Stop it. It's not funny," Emmy said from under her quilt. Suddenly they heard Pa's voice from the bottom of the stairs, "You two better be quiet. You don't want me to come up there."

Ma interrupted Pa, "And don't forget to say your prayers."

Emmy and Jake knelt beside Emmy's bed and said their prayers. Then, Emmy jumped back into her bed and pulled the quilt back over her head as fast as she could. Jake went to his bed without saying another word and listened to the night sounds.

The crackling fire was comforting. Once in awhile the wood hissed and then popped. Jake watched as a cinder flung itself onto the wooden floor only to burn itself out.

Outside his bedroom window, the snow tapped against the window. The light of the moon cast patterns while the tree branches brushed and swept the snow off time after time.

Once in a while, the echo of a wolf's cry mixed with the blowing wind. Jake tried to imagine what he would do if he met such an animal. He saw himself as a great hunter who took down this mighty beast. People came from everywhere to see his wolf. The ladies would pat him on his back and say, "Great Job! Were you scared?"

Jake would answer, "No!" and held up his wolf like a trophy for the world to see.

Morning came and the stories Pa told the night before faded into memory. Fresh snow lay on the ground and rabbit tracks were plenty. Jake asked his Pa if he could go rabbit hunting after his chores. Pa said, "Yes," but asked Jake to keep close to home. The sky and air gave warning that another storm was on its way.

Jake had just turned twelve years old and was considered a young man now. It was not unusual for a person his age to go out alone and help with the hunting, so the family had something to eat. Ma packed his lunch while he packed extra socks and ammunition. Jake was soon on his way to get some rabbits, so Ma could make rabbit stew for dinner.

As Jake followed the snow-covered tracks, he never gave heed to Pa's warning to stay close to home. He did not notice how dark the sky was getting. His feet throbbed from the bitter cold, so he stopped to put on another pair of socks and that's when Jake spotted his first rabbit.

Jake took hold of his rifle to shoot. He aimed but before Jake could shoot, he noticed something off to his right. It was the most beautiful creature Jake had ever seen. He thought it was some type of large dog.

Jake forgot about the rabbit as he studied this creature. The animal's legs were strong and lean, and his coat shone with many shades of gray, white, brown, and black. Jake thought this animal had become lost from last night's storm, so he called out to him, "Here boy."

The animal gazed at Jake deeply. Jake felt a sense of peace until he looked into the animal's yellow eyes and then it hit him. This creature had to be a wolf. Fear came over Jake as he remembered the stories Pa had told him. Jake's heart pounded a hundred miles a minute as he tried not to breathe. Jake thought, was my life about to end? My family… would I ever see them again?

Neither Jake nor the wolf moved a muscle or blinked an eye. Jake prayed for the wolf to leave, but the wolf just stood there. Jake and the wolf just stared at each other.

Jake thought … Why is this wolf just standing there staring at me? Is he sizing me up for his next meal? The wolf has his strength and strong teeth for his protection. I have my gun for my protection, but will my rabbit gun be enough to kill a huge wolf?

As time passed, Jake started to feel a bond toward the wolf. Jake imagined what it would be like if they played tag together. The wolf would run circles around him for a couple of minutes before allowing Jake to tag him. Once Jake tag the wolf, it was the wolf's turn to chase Jake. The wolf gave Jake a head start before running full force toward him. The wolf looked a locomotive engine coming down a track and unable to stop before the big hit. Jake pictured how it would feel if the wolf managed to take his front shoulder and clip him just behind his leg. His hit sent Jake to the ground.

Of course, in Jakes imagination the snow always cushioned his fall, so Jake was never hurt. Jake would lie in the snow to catch his breathe as the wolf continued run circles around him.

Jake pictured himself playing dead. He lay in the snow and waited for the wolf to come to him. Jake stayed very still until the wolf came close enough for him to grab onto the wolf's neck. Jake wouldn't let go. The two of them rolled in the snow together. The wolf waited for Jake to get up to start the chase all over again.

"What foolish thoughts," Jake told himself as the wind chilled his bones back to reality. The only thing Jake knew for sure was that one of them had to make the first move: Leave each other alone or attack. Jake did not want to be the one to move. But if the wolf decided to attack, Jake was ready with his gun.

Jake's bones and muscles were tired from being still for so long. He decided it wouldn't hurt if he moved his toes up and down in his boots or his shoulders back and forth under his wool coat. Jake though, a wolf couldn't see toes move in boots or shoulders move under a coat…Or could he?

The wolf turned his head just for a second to look over at a rabbit that dashed into a hole. His paws moved up and down a few times. After several minutes of a stare down, the wolf turned completely around and walked toward the woods.

Jake started to count to himself. One…Two…Three…The wolf walked three steps, turned back toward Jake's direction and stared at him.

"Look, neither one of us wanted to be here, so just go. I won't hurt you if you don't hurt me. Go…Just go and I will leave you alone." Jake mumbled to himself.

Jake had to do more than just wiggle his toes, move his shoulders and daydream about what it would be like to have a wolf as a friend, for the charley horse in his left leg became too painful. Jake closed his eyes and grab his leg as a loud scream blurted out of his mouth. "Aaaaah!"

When Jake opened his eyes, the wolf had vanished.

Dark clouds covered the sky and blocked out any warmth the sun had given earlier. Large snowflakes came down like chicken feathers in a pillow fight.

The snow turned into wet sleet. Jake had to cover his face for the ice felt like bee stings as it hit his face.

Jake was alone. The only sound was that of the wind when it whistled through the tree branches. Once in awhile chunks of snow fell off the branches. That was an eerie sound for each time a chunk of snow fell, Jake thought it was the footsteps of the wolf. Between the wind and the heavy wet snow, many of the trees could no longer stand straight. Draped in a blanket of snow, the smaller pine tree limbs bent toward the ground while some of the larger tree limbs snapped from the weight of the snow. Sometimes when a tree crashed, it took other trees with it. This broke the rhythm of the wind's whistle.

Jake knew he was lost when he came to an unfamiliar open field. Jake could only think of calling his Pa, so he screamed Pa's name as loud as he could. "Pa…Pa!" Jake listened for Pa's voice, but his Pa never called back. Jake's screams were muffled by the wind.

Jake's body shook and his hands and feet were numb. He had to get out of the cold. Jake started to dig a hole in which to hide. As he dug, he felt something nearby. Jake just knew someone, or something was there. He was afraid to look. "Pa is that you?" Jake asked. There was no response. Jake looked out toward the open field and there he noticed the faint outline of an animal. This time he knew the wolf had returned.

Unable to stand, Jake crawled away from the wolf. He screamed at him, "Get out of here! Go on!" As the wolf approached Jake, he inched away. With his gun in hand Jake screamed, "I've got you now."

The wolf just looked at Jake with his yellow eyes and stayed nearby. "Why are you still here? Can't you see that I have a gun and I can kill you?" Jake said. The wolf did not move.

Jake could feel the warmth of the wolf's breath upon his face. Too tired to get up, Jake inched his hand toward the wolf so he could touch him. The wolf backed away and howled. Jake knew if the wolf wanted to hurt him, he would have done so by now. Jake got up on his knees and reached out to touch the wolf. This time the wolf allowed Jake to place his arm around his neck.

The wolf's coat was warm. His muscles were lean yet strong. While Jake held onto the wolf, Jakes blood began to flow freely again. It was this warmth and strength that encourage Jake to get back on his feet and continue his journey toward home, but this time Jake had the help of a wolf.

Jake tried not to stumble, for each time he did, a low short howl, "Whooo," came from the wolf. Exhausted, Jake fell to his knees and cried. Jake looked up and shouted at the wolf, "It's no use. I can't go on!" The harder Jake cried the louder the wolf howled. Sometimes the wolf's howl pierced Jake's ears.

The wolf used a long, high pitched howl, "Whoooooo." It was the same high pitch sound Jake heard while lying in his bed at night. In between the wolf's howls, Jake could hear Pa's voice, "Jake…Jake, can you hear me?" Pa's voice became louder and louder each time he called Jake's name.

"Over here! Over here!" Jake screamed.

As Pa came nearer, the wolf licked Jake's face. It was as if his mother were drying away his tears. Then the wolf pulled away from Jake and was gone. Before Jake knew it, Pa stood over him, telling him they only had a short distance left to go home.

Ma helped Jake out of his wet clothes and into bed. Jake wanted to tell his Ma and Pa about the wolf, but he was afraid they would not believe him. Pa had always told him that wolves are evil. Jake wondered what would happen if he tried to tell Pa about his wolf? Would Pa call him a liar?

Jake had to go out and find his wolf and thank him for saving his life. He had to show Ma and Pa that wolves were not all bad. Jake needed to do it in such a way that they would not find out until he could show them the kindness of his wolf firsthand.

While in bed, Jake tried to think of a way he could bring his wolf home. He figured he could ask his Pa if he could go rabbit hunting in the morning. That evening, Jake thought about the journey he had with his wolf. As Jake listened to the wolf's howls in the distance, he knew that one day soon they would meet again.

Jake was up before the sun. He managed to complete his chores before Ma and Pa got up. After breakfast, Jake asked his Pa if he could go rabbit hunting. Jake told Pa that his chores were done, that he felt fine and the weather was going to be good.

Pa asked Jake to check with Ma to make sure that he didn't have a temperature before he could go out. Ma took his temperature twice to make sure that it was normal. Jake could not wait until he could get back outside to look for the wolf that had saved his life.

Jake packed up some food, extra socks and his gun. As he went out the door, Pa called out, "Don't be too late." Jake reassured his Pa that he would be home early. "Won't they be surprise when I bring a wolf home?" Jake mumbled to himself as he went out the door.

All morning and early afternoon Jake tracked his wolf. He even tried following his howls, but they stopped. With no luck, Jake had to return home. He had promised Pa that he would be home early.

When Jake reached the house, he noticed Pa was getting the horses ready to go into town. Pa could see that Jake was upset. Pa asked Jake if he wanted to go into town with him. Jake jumped at another chance to look for his wolf.

Jake helped Pa harness the horses and hooked them the sleigh. It was not long before the two of them were on their way into town. As they traveled, Jake kept his eyes and ears open. Pa asked Jake, "What's wrong with you today?"

Jake wanted to tell Pa about the wolf. He wanted to describe this mighty creature who had brought him home in that storm, but Jake couldn't find the words.

As the two made their way into the small village, they saw a large gathering of people. Men hooted and hollered, children laugh and yelled, "Come! Come quick!" Everyone was rushing over to the courthouse.

Jake asked Pa if he would stop the sleigh, so he could see what was happening. As soon as Pa was able to stop the horses, Jake ran toward the crowd. He screamed, "Let me see! Let me see!"

Jake managed to push his way to the front of the crowd. He stopped. His eyes could not believe what he saw. There, hanging lifeless from a wooden pole, was his wolf.

Hunters stood next to his wolf for a photo. One hunter growled as he took the wolf by the head so he could open and close its mouth like it was going to bite someone. Another hunter tried to show off Jake's wolf as if it were some kind of monster and a trophy to be had by all.

Jake wanted to shout out, "You monster!!! You monsters!!" but nothing came out. All Jake could do was stand there. He felt sick. He had to run. As Jake ran, the only thing he could think of was that maybe if he had told his story about the gentleness of wolves their shyness, this animal would not be a trophy for a hunter, but he had said nothing…nothing at all.

Pa caught up to Jake and asked him what was wrong, because Jake was sobbing like a child. The only words Jake could get out were, "You lied." Pa looked at him with bewilderment.

"What do you mean, son?" Pa asked.

"All the stories you told me about wolves are lies. Wolves are not horrible monsters that hurt and eat people." Jake said.

Pa took hold of Jake and said, "Son, I know you seen dead animals before, but what the world has…" before Pa could finish his sentence, Jake started yelling. "No, Pa listen to me. You're wrong about wolves! Last night during that storm the wolf that's hanging up back there saved my life. He brought me home, Pa. Can't you remember the loud howling that night? It was his strength and howls that kept me going and brought you out from the house, so you could find me."

The tears were running down Jake's cheeks. He was desperate for Pa to understand. Jake pierced Pa with his eyes, willing him to see what he had seen that night.

"Pa, that wolf tooth necklace around your neck…I remember asking you a long time ago why you kept it on all the time. You said it was to help you remember. Remember what?" Jake asked. The tension between them was great. Pa turned away from Jake. "Remember what, Pa?" Jake asked again.

As Pa turned around to face Jake, he could see the hurt in his Pa's eyes. That's when it hit Jake. "Pa…you knew! You knew the truth about wolves. Wolves aren't the monsters you made them out to be. Why, Pa? Why did you lie about wolves?"

Pa could hardly speak and the words he could get out were spoken softly. "I guess some fables were spun out to frighten young children who would wander from home, while other tales were made up to enhance a man's ego. That's all."

"That's all? That's all!" Jake screamed. Jake could not control the hurt and anger that he felt. "You're saying that you passed down stories to frighten children and to build yourself up? How could you, Pa? How could you let this happen? I believed in you. Look what happened to my wolf because of lies." Jake sobbed.

Pa reached into his trouser pocket and pulled out the silver piece he had won for his wolf. He took hold of Jake's hand and placed it into his palm and said, "Now, it's your turn to remember son."

Pa put his arm around Jake's shoulder and led him back to the sleigh to go home.

As they assed the courthouse, Jake held the coin Pa has given him and took one last glimpse at the wolf that had saved his life, while the last word Pa told him kept running through his mind… REMEMBER… REMEMBER…

PROFILE OF THE WOLF

<u>Scientific Name</u>: Canis Lupus

<u>Size</u>: 25 to 38 inches at the shoulder

<u>Voice</u>: Long low to high pitch howls. Low howls to growl. Most of the time wolves will howl to bring the family together and mark their territory. Pups must be very careful when they howl when lost. This may bring death to the pup from another pack.

<u>Color</u>: Ranges from Black to blond, often gray upper body over gray chest.

<u>Habitat</u>: Usually lives in forested area and may travel 40 miles a day.

Usually travels in Packs of 3 to more than 20. Composed of a family member and led by an alpha male and female who mate for life. The whole pack takes on the responsibility of raising the pups. Each pup is encouraged to develop its stronger trait, whether the pup is an omega or alpha.

<u>Litter Size</u>: 4-6 pups.

<u>Food</u>: Wolves are predators (meat eaters). The average adult wolf consumes 5-10 pounds of meat a day. They like elk, deer, bison, mountain sheep, marmots, mice, squirrels, rabbit, beavers and fish. In a few cases they have been known to go after livestock when no other food is available.

WOLF FACTS

In 1974 the wolf received protection under the federal Endangered Species Act of 19973, making it illegal for citizens to kill wolves. This step was taken to preserve the few hundred that were left throughout the United States. Today, there are less than 300 red wolves left world.

To date, according to the U.S. Fish and Wildlife Services, there has never been a documented case in the United States of a healthy wolf (hybrids and pets are not included in this study) ever attacking or biting a human in over a 100 year.

Although the state Department of the Fish and Game assumed day-to-day management of wolves from the U.S. Department of Interior, the federal government still assists the states with wolf predator control. Wolves have been killed legally due to preying on livestock, but more dogs have killed livestock than wolves.

Several studies have shown the importance of the wolf to our ecosystem. Even with this in mind, very few people, organizations or Government agencies are fighting to keep the wolves from extinction.

By the late 1900's and early 2000's, the gray wolf was said to have made a comeback in places. This means that the gray wolf totals the number that each state feels it can support. This number is usually between 300-400 wolves, and in some states this number is much lower. There are only about a dozen or so states that have wolves.

The Federal Government is under pressure by local farmers and hunters wanting to de-classify the gray wolf from "endanger" to "threatened." The reason for this action is to make it legal for controlled hunting. In some states where the gray wolf has reached its maximum number, the state has controlled hunting.

Controlled hunting is a way to keep the wolf from going over the maximum number set by the state. An example of this is in Alaska. Alaska allows aerial hunting on its wolves to control population. This is how it works: A plane tracks down and chases the wolf until they can no longer run. Once the wolves are too tired to run, then they are shot.

  Get the facts. Learn about the habits and plight of the wolf by going to your local library and internet sites like: www.fws.gov/alligatorriver/redwolf.html and www.google.com and under search type: Endangered Species wolf.

  Be an ambassador to the wolf. Don't let innocent animals die due to human anger, ignorance and fairy tales.

www.ingramcontent.com/pod-product-compliance
Lightning Source LLC
Chambersburg PA
CBHW042036120526

44592CB00028B/72